Sales Simplified

Understanding the Basics

William J. Simpson

© 2014 William J Simpson.
All Rights Reserved Worldwide.

ISBN-13: 978-1497507777
ISBN-10: 1497507774

Published by
'If, And or But' Publishing Company
P.O. Box 2559
Battle Creek, Michigan 49016 USA
www.ifandorbutpublishing.com

No part of this publication may be replicated, redistributed, transmitted, or given away in any form or by any means mechanical or electronic without the prior written consent of the publisher and/or author as relayed to you herein. This includes photocopying or recording or by any storage or information retrieval device or email.

The information and views in this book are those of the author alone and should not be taken as expert instruction or command. The reader is responsible for his or her own actions in using or applying the data herein. Neither the author nor publisher assume any liability or responsibility whatsoever on behalf of the purchaser and/or reader of the material.

Acknowledgments:

Special Acknowledgment to my father: Bill Simpson. For the help on the editing, revisions and ideas that led to a successful production.

To my mom, family and Christine for believing in me through my life and professions!

&

To all those who make a living in sales!
May this help take you to new levels of success!

Table of Contents

Introduction..1
Chapter One: *Goooooaaaaaaaaal!*...5
Chapter Two: Where's Your Head?..11
Chapter Three: Work Time...17
Chapter Four: Energize!...19
Chapter Five: Don't Lose Your Cool!.......................................23
Chapter Six: Positive over Negative.......................................27
Chapter Seven: Show and Tell..29
Chapter Eight: Curiosity and the Cat......................................31
Chapter Nine: Story Time..35
Chapter Ten: Building Blocks..37
Chapter Eleven: Stay in Control..39
Chapter Twelve: Detour Ahead...43
Chapter Thirteen: You're So Pretty!.......................................47
Chapter Fourteen: My Dog Ate my Homework!!!..................49
Chapter Fifteen: I know you are, but what am I?..................53
Chapter Sixteen: My Finger Slipped.......................................57
Chapter Seventeen: More or Less?..63
Chapter Eighteen: I swear... True Story!...............................65
Chapter Nineteen: "I'll think about it"....................................67
Chapter Twenty: 'Tag' me in..71
Chapter Twenty-One: Cash or Credit?...................................73
Chapter Twenty-Two: For just $40 more!..............................77
Chapter Twenty-Three: "My Dad's better than your Dad!"......79
Chapter Twenty-Four: Homework!...85
Chapter Twenty-Five: Who Are You?.....................................89
Chapter Twenty-Six: Additional Data.....................................91
Chapter Twenty-Seven: Cheat Sheet.....................................93

About the Author..97

Introduction

Sales are an incredible tool in everyone's life. Whether you think you are good at sales or bad at sales, at one point in your life, you have "sold" something. It could be huge, like a multi-million dollar company, something smaller, a car, even smaller, a product at the local fair or even smaller than that, when you talked your friends into going to see that movie you wanted to see. At one point or another, you have sold something.

I have found that there are levels of sales. Someone who can talk to their friends and talk them into doing something but who doesn't really like talking to people they don't know.

There is the "salesman" professional who makes their living selling items. This type has no problem talking to people.

There is also what I like to call the "natural". This person may have no sales training or tons of sales training. This person can talk to anybody at any time and naturally sell him or her something. It doesn't matter if they know the product or if it's their first time seeing the product. They can sell it because they have a natural ability to talk to people and it may not even seem like they are "selling."

The one thing that all these people have in common is, they can all sell. They may not realize it but every person in the world can sell. With the proper tools and the proper outlook, anyone can sell. This book will give you many tools to use in your life, profession and everyday dealings and when used correctly, will hopefully bring you as much success as it has brought me!

A lot of things are misunderstood when it comes to sales so I will define them now:

>**Sale:** This is when an item is exchanged with another item of equal value to each party (this item of equal value could be money).

>**Pitch** (*Short for Sales Pitch*): This is a type of promotion that involves a demonstration.

Control: This is defined as the ability to influence or direct something or someone towards some item, goal or destination.

Close: This is a very misunderstood word in sales. A close in a sales pitch is simply a stop. It can also be the completion of a sale where goods have been exchanged. We will delve into this more later.

Attention: This is simply where you're putting your focus.

Interest: This is the action of being genuinely curious and wanting to learn about something.

Interesting: This is creating curiosity or attracting the attention of someone or something. An object, music, conversation or even a person can be interesting.

These are very important words and when understood, will benefit you greatly in all of your sales and in life. A very important thing to remember when you are selling, learning, or reading anything, make sure to define any words you do not understand.

This is one thing to truly remember when you are selling a product. You want to make sure that you understand all about that product including related items that could possibly come up.

For example, if you are an Architect and a potential client comes up and asks what you would design the north elevation to look like, but you don't understand what a "north elevation" is, it would be difficult to handle that question since you do not understand the question fully.

Now to clarify that point, in Architecture, the word "elevation" designates the surface of something. It can relate to inside or exterior walls or even cabinets.

So, in the example, the "North Elevation" would be the north wall of the building. Knowing this seems pretty crucial if you were going to make it as an Architect. This applies in every profession, no matter how small or large it is.

When you decide to be involved in something new make sure to define all words you do not fully understand as this will help you dramatically in the long run.

Chapter One:

Gooooooaaaaaaaal!

Targets are essential when in sales. If you don't have a target or a goal you will find that your sales are much lower than if you set a target.

A Target is defined as: *a goal, destination, purpose, or objective that you are aiming for.*

In the sense of sales, it is a number, or amount of product you are trying to reach or sell.

Now there can be many different types of targets. You can have a yearly target, monthly target, weekly target, a daily target, and even an hourly target.

A lot of people establish a few of these targets but not necessarily all of them. You will find when you establish all of the above targets you will find it much easier to reach them.

Each one of the targets is a sub-product of the other. Let's look at them one by one, starting from the top:

> **Yearly Target:** A yearly target is the goal or objective you want to make in a year.
>
> **Monthly Target:** This is the target for each month that you would have to reach to make your yearly target. Yearly target divided by 12.
>
> **Weekly Target:** This is the target you would have to reach each week to make your monthly target. Now as each month does not have the same amount of weeks you would have to arrange accordingly.
>
> **Daily Targets:** This is the target you would have to reach each day to make your weekly targets. You would just have to figure it out accordingly to fit with the days you are going to work on the project.

Hourly Targets: These are targets you have to reach each hour to make your daily targets. Again this has to be according to the number of hours you are working on the project. These targets are very good when in sales, specifically small item sales, things that can be sold many times each hour.

Now for an example, we will use a simple example, let's say you are selling books.

> **Yearly Target:** 8320 books
>
> **Monthly Target:** 694 (8320 divided by 12 and rounded up)
>
> **Weekly Target:** 160 (8320 divided by 52, if you are working every week)
>
> **Daily Target:** 32 (160 divided by 5, five day work week rounded up)
>
> **Hourly Target:** 4 (32 divided by 8 hours a day)

Now looking at the top number, that's a lot of books. However as you break it down the number gets smaller and smaller until it's a real, obtainable number. Breaking down your targets makes the outrageous number, obtainable.

This system works well for almost any product. However depending on what your product is you will have to adjust the numbers accordingly. And certain products would have to have sub-targets.

Let's take car sales:

> **Yearly Target:** 96 cars
>
> **Monthly Target:** 8 cars
>
> **Weekly Target:** 2 cars (rounded up)
>
> **Daily Target:** 40 people talked to
>
> **Hourly Target:** 5 people contacted (8 hour days)

Now another main point that is very vital on sales is the target that you set. Always set your target much higher than what you are shooting for. For this targeting system to work, you actually have to shoot for that target like it is your only target. Do not shoot for "bare minimum."

I have found that increasing your target by 50% works well. For example if you want to sell 96 cars in a year, add 50% to that and base your targets on the bigger target.

This way you can really work hard to make those targets and this allows you to shoot for a way bigger number. Now you actually have to shoot for the bigger target. Don't just hit your minimum targets then stop working. Keep selling!

In targeting there is one more point that comes into play: Obtainable targets. If you continuously set outrageous unobtainable targets, or someone sets them for you, you can start to feel defeated. This is not good for a sales person, or anyone for that matter. The key is to set reasonably obtainable targets; not so low that you don't have to hustle, but they also can't be so high that they are only possible if a miracle occurs.

This is what separates the salesman from the every day seller. It separates the people who make the "big bucks" from the people that are just getting by in sales. If you set targets, make them bigger and never stop pushing to make those targets, and when you make them, keep selling!!! This will allow you to flourish and prosper and be above them all!

Not all days will be great sales days so get all the sales you can when you have the chance. Don't just sit back and relax because you made today's target. Next week, you could have little or no sales and you'll be glad you were ahead of your target. "Make hay when the sun shines!" as they say.

Chapter Two:

Where's your head?

Ever been talking to someone and realize that you're not sure what you were talking about? You were on autopilot and had a full conversation but you can't remember a thing that was said? Or in sales, you did an entire sales pitch to a customer and came to a point where you realized you weren't sure what was next? This happens a lot and you would be very surprised how common it actually is.

Every person in the world has a certain amount of attention that they can spread around before they cannot pay attention to anything more. Some people have more than others. This is not a bad thing, just a thing to be aware of.

For example, if you are driving a car. You are paying attention to the road, to the other drivers around you, and to the lights, whether they're green, yellow or red. Most people can do that.

Now someone calls you. Now you're also on the phone while driving. Less people can do this safely. Let's now add eating. Even less people can do that, and certainly, not safely. Let's add one more thing, your car is a manual and you are in traffic. This is extremely hard and shouldn't be tried by anyone. You may be able to do it, but it's not wise and may result in an accident. I do not recommend it.

Doing all this puts your attention quite thin. It is much harder than just simply driving the car. No phones, no food. Just driving. Why is this? Because your attention is completely on driving, there's nothing else to worry about.

This applies to sales also. Attention is very important. You want all of your attention on the customer in front of you. You don't want it on the customer and on last week when you went to see that movie. You will find that when your attention is not simply on the customer in front of you, you will run into things you aren't ready to handle. You'll forget what you were saying to the customer and repeat yourself, etc.

This applies even farther. Let's say you're

starving or dehydrated and you're talking to a customer. Your stomach is growling and you really need to eat. Your attention is on yourself and not on the customer, at least not fully. Let's say the customer asks a question that would have been easy to handle if all your attention were available. But now it's suddenly annoying and you find yourself getting irritated. Result... Sale lost.

The one thing to think about is, you are there to sell. You are there to make a lot of money! You are there to make sure the customer gets a quality product which is exactly what they want. The way to do this is to make sure you have all of your attention on sales. Don't be concerned with the last sale that you couldn't close, or the customer yesterday who pissed you off.

The entirety of your attention should be on the customer in front of you or the customers who will be coming. Let's say you are waiting for a customer. A lot of pitch products, which you will find at trade-shows, small and large, are reliant on a lot of customers walking by.

Sometimes at these shows the traffic will slow down. This does not mean that there are no customers. Do not start talking with fellow sales people or the vendors next to you. Because as soon as you do that you will miss the one customer coming by that would have purchased your product.

This has happened to me before and I learned quickly. The traffic had slowed down dramatically and I started chatting it up with a vendor. Another salesman was with me and he called the one customer over that I would have talked to had I not been talking to the vendor. This customer proceeded to buy $400 of the product I was selling. At that time I was working strictly on commission so that was a big sale to miss.

Where was my attention? On the vendor. Not on the customers still walking around the convention. Time and time again I have been rewarded for simply keeping my attention on finding the next customer, and not putting it on other things, like other salesman or vendors, or my friend's birthday party I went to last week and how much fun we had.

You will find that this applies to many other things in life too. If your attention is on the thing you want, you will find that it will be that much easier to acquire than if you have your attention on many other things.

The main point of this is to keep your attention on the customers in front of you, not on your last customer, not on the dinner you had with your family the night before, just the customer in front of you.

Try this, talk to every customer like it was your first time talking to any customer, but with all the knowledge you have currently about the product you are selling.

16 ~ Sales Simplified: *Understanding the Basics*

Chapter Three:

Work Time

Customers are the sole thing that sales rely on. Sales do not rely on the boss, or the dog, or the food you eat. Sales would not exist without customers. Sales do not occur without customers. Luckily customers are very common anywhere in life. There will always be someone to sell, anywhere you go, and that's why sales are an ever-growing industry. Without sales, no company would survive, no transactions would occur.

However, one person cannot sell for 24 hours a day, 7 days a week. This is why successful sales people are completely focused on sales when it is work time.

A lot of people go to work and chat, socialize, and goof off during work hours. If these people are in sales, they will not survive. They probably work on commission, may have a minimal base but most of their pay is based on the commissions on their sales. When you are at work, focus on work. Focus on your target and making every hour count. You should of course enjoy your work, hopefully, so this does not mean you shouldn't have fun. But remember your pay is directly related to sales. If you make a lot of sales, you make a lot more money, if you don't make sales, you won't make money. It's as simple as that.

The people in sales who make the most in the industry are the people who come to work ready to sell. They are ready to make their targets and surpass them. They are ready to learn more about the product they sell and they are focused on work during the time that they are at work. These people are the one's who make huge commissions. These are the people who make a ton of money.

Remember that you only have a certain amount of time to sell, don't waste it talking to vendors, friends, fellow sales people, etc. Focus on sales and the customers you have. Why waste them?

Chapter Four:

Energize!

When a customer comes to look at your product or is interested in your product, he or she is interested in learning about the product. They are not coming over to hear about your bad mood or hear you complain about life. They are coming to learn about the product. Being in a bad mood or complaining about something or simply not paying attention to them will lose your sale and a customer.

When you are in sales, you want to be approachable, smiling, and encouraging. Now, there is a difference, you want to be genuinely happy; fake happy, is not happy and although your customer may not know it, they can sense it.

Have you ever gone to buy something and you could tell that all the sales person wanted to do was to sell you? They really didn't care what you actually wanted. Now think of another situation where you went to buy something and you could tell the sales person actually cared about you and wanted to help you get what you wanted. That is the difference. When you are in sales, you want to actually care about the customer and what he or she wants. Being in a bad mood will prevent that.

If you are in a bad mood, or had a bad day, you can create a façade that shows enthusiasm. Now this has to be done to a point where you yourself believe you are enthusiastic. Faking enthusiasm is easily seen through. However, if you genuinely create the enthusiasm to a point where you yourself believe that you are in a good mood, you will start selling and suddenly, you will actually be happy and enthusiastic.

In sales, be encouraging, enthusiastic and just simply in a good mood, and your sales will be a lot higher. Customers like talking to someone who is obviously having fun, likes their job, and enjoys talking to people. No one wants to talk to a depressed, angry person.

Overall, be happy, energetic and smile! Have fun in your job. Meeting new people is fun, especially when you make them that much happier after talking to you and giving them what they need! It's a great feeling to see a customer leave happier than when they arrived!

Chapter Five:

Don't lose your cool!

In sales, people are going to get frustrated. Sales people will get agitated, pissed off, annoyed and downright infuriated some times. Customers are not perfect. They will do things that will irritate you, whether they are intending to or not.

Let's say you are having a rough day, sales are low and you are not making your goals. Then a customer comes along; you spend a ton of time with them and they walk away and don't buy. That can push you over the edge to the point of boiling over and you may even take it out on the customer....

Don't do this!

It will not help your sales in the least. Getting frustrated, pissed off or just generally angry with customers will harm your sales in the short and long run. Not to mention if you get mad at a customer or are rude to them, it hurts the company's image too. The one thing you have to realize is people are just that, people. They're not all going to buy. Some will need to think about it, some won't buy immediately but will buy later. Some will need to "mull it over". In sales, this will happen. Some customers actually have "rules" that they will not buy anything the first time looking or seeing the product. They need to "walk around" or "see reviews" first.

If you are having a hard day with customers getting on your nerves, the worst thing you can do is get frustrated or upset. It is a dwindling spiral. Once you get frustrated you will continue to get more and more upset and your sales will never improve. It just gets worse and worse.

The handling: as soon as you start to get frustrated, leave the area, take a walk and get some fresh air. Get your attention off sales for a minute and go outside to cool off. Look at things around you. Look at the people around you until you feel better and you can find something you like about people again. Once you feel better, return to sales and you will find that sales come better and easier.

The best thing you can do in sales is to operate as explained in the previous chapter. Every customer is different. Every customer has different needs. Every customer even has an entirely new demeanor.

The best way to handle customers, new or old, is like he or she is your friend and you want to help them. Some will find this easier than others, but, if you can master this, you will do great in sales. Just remember, you rely on good customer relations.

If you have a bad attitude towards customers, how is that going to work in the long run? Not very good. You may lose the sale now, and lose a potential customer for life. Besides, how is getting frustrated going to benefit you in any way? So why do it in the first place.

Another big point in sales is what you think of yourself. If you have the idea that all sales people are con artists or scammers, then that's what you are going to give off to customers. You have to remember, if you genuinely want to help people and assist in the betterment of their life, then you are going to do great. When you believe in yourself, people can believe in you.

26~ Sales Simplified: *Understanding the Basics*

Remember you, yourself are the tool you use to do your job! Keep your cool and watch the sales roll in!

Chapter Six:

Positive over Negative

As I said above, being positive, energetic and encouraging is extremely vital in sales. Remember, faking it is not what I am talking about. Being natural and sincere is key.

One thing that will come naturally when you are being up-beat with customers, is body language. When you are giving your customer information, it is very important to have good body language. Naturally nod your head when you want them to agree with you on something. Don't stand there shaking your head at them un-naturally or you will look silly. But when you really believe something and you're telling someone who is interested, you will naturally do this, although you may not notice. Pay attention one time, you'll be amazed at how this occurs naturally.

You will also notice that when you are being positive you will have better eye-contact, control and better communication with your customers.

When you get a chance, go to a place where products are being sold: a trade-show, flea market, a fair, etc. Walk around and look at the sales people. Make observations about them. Look at their posture, their face; find someone who is talking to someone and notice how they are interacting with the customer. A lot of sales people would be shocked at how they actually look when talking to customers. A lot of times they wear their "weight" on their face. You could probably, by just looking at the sales people, tell who is having a good or bad day.

I once corrected a seller by videoing them. She wasn't selling well. I did a video of her while she was with a customer, without her noticing. Once she was done with the customer I took her aside and showed her the video. She was shocked by what she saw. She hadn't smiled once to the customer. She was slumped and didn't look like she enjoyed anything. After correcting her, she sold her very next customer.

Simple things like body language, if corrected will help your sales dramatically. The key is to be aware!

Chapter Seven:

Show and Tell

When a customer is interested in a product, they have not decided to buy it yet, or maybe they have. Either way, they will want to see it, how it works, what it does, how long it last, what's needed to maintain it, etc.

This is why showing a product and giving the customer any and all information they want and need is very vital.

Having a customer feel a product, hold it, move it, use it (in the sense of technology), etc. is an easy way to get the customer comfortable with the product. It is also a good way to add control in the sale.

(Example: selling skin care)

Sales Person: *"Here you go, hold this jar, check out the ingredients. Isn't that awesome? Now feel your hands. Doesn't it feel good on your skin?"*

This helps the customer to get an actual understanding of the product. It's much better than just telling them about the product. Now they actually have the physical thing in front of them and all the data you are telling them.

This works with all products. Have the customer feel or touch the product, work with the product or at a minimum, see the product. This will make all the difference in some sales and will help you close many more sales.

Chapter Eight:

Curiosity and the cat

We all know what happened to the cat when it got curious. Now this also applies in sales, in a sense of course. Earlier in this book we defined what interest and interesting are. These two words are directly related to sales.

When a customer comes to you, what are they interested in? The answer is simple. Your product! Not you. Not your life's activities. Not your bad mood. They are interested in your product.

These are commonly misunderstood in sales. A sales person can get so caught up in his own life that he can forget that his main priority at his job is to sell his product. Not talk about his life or other things. It is simply to interest the customer in the product and to sell the product.

What you want is to be interested in your customer. Find out their wants and needs; find out why they need this product. Find out what peaked their interest. Give them more data on the product that is applicable to them.

The key is, you want to know about them and what their wants and needs are. They're not there to hear what you had for breakfast, or that you just adopted a puppy. Remember you are there to sell, not have a conversation over coffee.

When you are interested in your customer you will find that sales happen more often and faster. You are finding out about your customer and are able to handle their wants and needs better. The other thing that happens when you are interested in your customer is you start to care about them.

This is a good thing because then you are able to relate to them better and give them what they need better. Some ways to be interested in your customer are to find things about the customer that you like or can relate to. This will make your interest genuine and will get the customer more comfortable with you.

Examples of someone trying to create interest and someone being interested in something are:

A Comedian is creating interest. He is doing things, which is making you laugh, or not. But your attention is fully on him because he is doing things that is pulling your attention. The audience is interested in him.

A parent who is listening to his kids' story of how they conquered the playground is interested in his kids and is giving them their full attention.

This is how a sales person should always operate. Listen to your customer, find out more about them and enlighten them on the product. Don't distract them by telling them non sequitur stories that do not relate to the product.

Being interested will help you far more than just in sales. Think of a few examples in your life that would have been better if you gave your attention to the situation rather than tried to pull the attention to yourself.

Chapter Nine:

Story Time

Most products in the world will help people make their life easier. Some are smaller than others but most products will help a person in one-way or another. A doll helps the over worked mom have some time for herself while her daughter plays with the doll. A lawn mower helps the man cut the yard rather than having to trim every blade of grass. A crane helps build the bridges that make things more accessible. The point is, everything, small and large, has a purpose.

In sales, your job is to make the product you are selling valuable to the customer. People will not (most of the times) buy something that they do not see any value in. Whether the value is small or large, no value to the customer means, no sales for you. So, when talking to customers you need to find the value of the product for them that will make their life easier. When you get them to realize value, suddenly you just made a sale.

Think about it this way, could you sell a car to a person who has 5 cars? Probably not. Or could you? Let's look at this example. A customer owns 5 cars, yet he is looking at cars. Your job, as a seller is to find out why and how to create value.

You find out, he has 5 cars, and they all get bad gas mileage. He doesn't need 5 cars but he has kept them for a long time. His family consists of himself, his wife, and two children, so you know he needs a larger car.

Maybe, he needs a van or SUV. His kids don't drive yet so no need to keep more than 2 cars. You show him a car that fits his whole family, gets great gas mileage, has all the upgrades and he is able to trade in 3 of his cars as a down payment so his cost would be very minimal.

Suddenly you have created value and made a sale.

Now maybe none of your sales will be like this but you can see how in this example, as long as you create value you can sell anyone. You just have to find enough value!

Chapter Ten:

Building Blocks

The Main Issue

When a customer is interested in a product or item, they usually have a reason or a few, but there is always a key reason. Whether or not they will tell you, is your job, as a seller, to find out.

If you are interested rather than interesting, you will find out the reason a lot faster. The difficulty will be based on the product you are selling and the reason they have for buying it. The more personal the reason, the more the customer will have to feel comfortable with you. The less personal, the easier it will be to learn the reason.

For example, if you are selling a car, the reason may simply be, "My old one broke down." However if you're selling a cream or other healing product, the reason may be embarrassing to the customer. So you have to really be interested in your customer and show them that they can trust you. This must be genuine. If you aren't genuine then you should not be in sales. Customers deserve to be treated with respect and your job, as a seller, is to help them.

The main issue, if found will allow you to really help your customer and give them all the information they need and sell them what they need rather than sell them something they do not need. Also as in the above chapter, finding the main issue will create value, as usually you can relate the product to the main issue and really help the customer.

Now, let's say that the customer doesn't have a "main reason." This will be very rare but it can happen. Let's say that they're just curious. If this occurs you can still sell them, you just have to create enough value in the product that they want to buy it.

Simply find the key reason the customer is interested in the product and watch your sales keep growing!

Chapter Eleven:

Stay in Control

Control

Control is a very key factor in sales. If you are constantly told what to do or you only do what your customer says, you will not sell them. Control is a huge tool in sales. Control is having someone do something that you want him or her to do.

Now there are two types of control:

- *The type of control that helps a person in their life.*
- *The type of control that does not benefit a person.*

1) The first type of control leads a person to an item, place or product that will help them in their life and promotes their survival. For example: a guy comes to buy a car, he is interested in the cheapest model but you are able to get him to buy a much more reliable car that will last him much longer and will not fail on him, and you are able to sell it to him in his price range. This would be control used to benefit someone.

2) The other type of control leads a person to an item, place or product that will not benefit them in their life. For example, consider the above example but change it to: The sales person forces a guy to buy a car that he can't afford which makes him unable to pay his bills rather than selling him the car he can afford.

In selling products, control is a very key thing. You control the sale. You just have to make sure that the end result is going to benefit the customer. As long as the things you are doing are adding to the survival of the customer, you will be helping them. You will also get a much better response and your sales will increase.

Examples of control:

- Let's say you sell a high quality skin cream: Have them hold the jar and read the ingredients. "Here, look at the ingredients." Then, hand the customer the jar. You can also have them feel their hands multiple times when they have put the product on (that is assuming your product feels good on the skin).

- Let's say you sell shoes at a mall. Have the customer sit down and actually put the shoes on. Then have them walk around in the shoes.

- If you sell cars, have the person test drive the car. Sit in the car. Touch the car. Press buttons in the car.

This all sounds very simple, but all of this is control. It gets the person doing what you want them to do. But it also gets the customer familiar with the product. They are able to actually experience the product, which is extremely valuable as they will develop a liking-ness to the product or they won't, and this will allow you to find what they truly like.

If you were to ask anyone, "Do you like being controlled?" You would probably get a unanimous response of, "NO!" However, if you told them that being controlled, in small ways, would greatly increase their survival, you would most likely get a, "Yes."

Control, if beneficial, is not a bad thing and is often greatly misunderstood. If you really look at your life, you use control all the time, and you are controlled in a good way all the time. Small and large, control is not a bad thing.

Just make sure you are not using control that harms people as this, in the end will harm you and the people around you. A real easy example of this is: Street Lights. They control you by controlling the flow of traffic. Can you imagine if there were no streetlights or method of traffic control? How chaotic would that be? Insanity.

Chapter Twelve:

Detour Ahead

In sales, the entire purpose is to sell the customer. That is the valuable final product. The sale. Now many products are sold in different ways. You have large purchases, medium purchases, small purchases, pitch products, and even buy-now products. Each product has its own way of being sold. Large and medium products usually take time to sell.

For example, cars, or expensive software, are things you may only sell 5-25 a month. Then, there are smaller products, pitch products and buy-now's, which you may sell 10-200 in a day. However, each one is sold in generally the same way.

A customer comes over interested in your product, you tell them about it, get them interested in the product and then they buy the product. Those are the basic steps of a sale. But the most important point in each of these steps is making sure the customer stays on track. You have heard the phrase before: the quickest way from point A to point B is a straight line. This actually applies to sales.

When a customer is showing interest in your product, you can talk and talk and talk with that customer without ever selling them. End result, you spent a lot of time with a potential customer but never closed the sale. That is no good.

The point I am trying to make here is to keep the customers on track. This is not to say that you don't talk with the customer or learn about them, this is simply saying just keep your mind on where you want this customer to end up. Closed.

If a customer starts veering from the line, simply let them finish talking, acknowledge them and then bring them back to the sale. If they say something that is pertinent to the sale, listen and remember what they said, as it may be useful later on in the close, but always keep them on track.

Example (a customer is interested in buying a dishwasher):

Sales Person: *"Here is our two top brands for a reasonable price, dishwasher A as a few more options than dishwasher B but it is slightly more expensive..."*

Customer: *"My mom had a dishwasher like dishwasher B. She said it works very well."*

Sales Person: *"That's good. It is a very good dishwasher, very reliable and will clean your dishes extremely well!"*

Customer: *"That's good. My mom is actually very funny, one time she was putting dishes in the dishwasher and had to go to the bathroom, when she came back the cat had gotten into the dishwasher. It was hysterical!"*

Sales Person: *"Wow!!! That is too funny! I can't believe that happened. Luckily with this dishwasher, if it's open, it won't turn on, so if that were to happen, no harm would come to the animal. Also it has an emergency shut off on the side just in case it's needed."*

Customer: *"Oh that's cool. What else can it do...?"*

See? The customer started to pull away from the conversation. Granted it was about the product in general, but this happens all the time. The sales person, in the example, could have easily gone on a tangent and started talking about his own cat, but instead, he was able to FULLY acknowledge the customer.

As a result, the customer didn't feel interrupted or that the salesperson wasn't interested in them. Then the salesperson was able to return the customer back to the product at hand.

You will see this happen with all products. Customers will change subjects, or start telling you a story. It's not a bad thing. This is actually a good sign. It means they are getting comfortable with you. However, you do not want to allow it to get out of hand as you will end up losing the sale because they got distracted and lost interest in the product.

The point is simply keeping the customers on the correct path to the desired end, and that end is, the Close!

Chapter Thirteen:

You're so pretty!

As everyone likes to feel good about them self, compliments work very well in sales. Sincere compliments work the best as fake compliments are, well, fake. Now that's not saying that every second of the sale you want to be complimenting the customer, you have to do it in the right way, and too many compliments make you seem fake. But flattery works very well.

If a customer has a cool thing they're wearing, or told you a cool story, acknowledge them appropriately. A lady has a cool ring on, "that's a beautiful ring." A guy drives a nice car, "that's a really cool car." A couple tells you how they met and it's very romantic, tell them so.

Sometimes it's very obvious when a customer comes over, what they are proud of. Show them you noticed by mentioning something that you liked about it. It's a small point, but it works. Compliments, flattery, etc. don't leave home without it!

Chapter Fourteen:

My dog ate my homework!!!

"Stories, not lies"

If a customer is not closing, it is usually because they do not see enough value in the product yet. Tell them success stories of other customers with the product. The best stories will be stories that are relevant to why the customer is interested. For example, in the sense of skin products, if the customer is interested in the product for eczema, tell them success stories of customers who got benefits using the product on eczema.

Another key point on stories is, be specific. The more specific you are with the data, the more the customer will benefit from it. If you tell a customer, "Oh Yeah, he used it for eczema and loved it." That's nice and all, but it isn't enough. "Oh eczema, yeah I had a customer who bought this product last year, used it for 3 months and saw differences, continued to use it and in 6 months it was practically cleared up, he actually came back and bought more recently" (if that's true).

"Prove yourself to your customer three times and they will trust you."

To elaborate on the above, when a customer comes over, you are a stranger selling a product they may know nothing or something about. Most of the times, people selling products do not really understand the product and are just simply trying to sell a product. A good sales person knows to learn and understand his product. When you are selling a product, in order for you to get a customer to trust you and believe what you are saying, you have to be able to prove it.

How do you do that? Well it's a little simpler than you think. Let's take our car example:

> **Customer:** "How much gas mileage does this car get?"
>
> **Salesman:** "21 city, 31 highway. Here are some documents showing that the car gets between 20-23 city and 30-33 highway. I also just sold a few of these cars and had

the customers give me their opinions and here is what they said about the gas mileage." Shows customer the reviews from his other customers, verifying the gas mileage.

That's 1. I'm sure you can think of two more examples for the product you sell. Proving yourself does not have to be complicated. It simply needs to show proof that you know what you're talking about. And the magic number happens to be three.

If you prove yourself three times, customers will be more likely to believe the next thing you say without much proof. This is NOT saying that you can or should lie to a customer, which is one thing I am not trying to teach. I believe that you should always tell a customer the truth!

This is just teaching you that you should always prove yourself to each customer you talk to. It will make your sales easier and it will make your customers trust and feel comfortable with you.

Chapter Fifteen:

I know you are but what am I?

Being Right:

Everyone has heard the phrase, "The Customer is Always Right." This is a true and false statement. In the end it is more true than false. However, there is more to it than just that.

Everyone wants to "be right." It is just how everyone is. As a seller, you should really know your product. You may know it so well that you know more than anyone, especially the customer. The customer obviously doesn't know all about the product or they wouldn't want more information, *right?*

Wrong. In today's world, information on pretty much everything is readily available. Your cell phone, your laptop or tablet, any information about everything is available at the touch of a button and most customers research products before they purchase. They compare, get reviews, and learn about your specific product and about your competitors.

When a customer comes up to you, interested in your product, do not assume that they know nothing. Assume that they know something and you are just giving them more data. One of the biggest mistakes a seller can make is to tell a customer that he or she is wrong. What will happen is exactly what happens to most people, they will "puff-up" and assert their rightness, even if they know that they could be wrong. It's just what most people do (this will not occur 100% of the time, but its best just to avoid it).

If you are telling a customer about a product and the customer interjects something that disagrees with what you said, the correct handling is to acknowledge the customer and handle it accordingly without making the customer or yourself wrong.

For example: A person goes to buy a car,

> **Salesman:** *"The 2002 model gets 38 MPG highway and 34 City."*

Customer: *"No, this car gets 34 highway and 30 city, I did my research before I came and that's what I found."*

This is the point where the seller can completely mess up the sale or save it. The customer has done his research and knows about this car. There are two scenarios here.

#1 (Wrong way) Seller: "You don't know what you're talking about. I have been selling this car since it came out. I know what it gets."

This will mess up the sales cycle, the customer is made-wrong and the sale will most likely be lost. The customer will then assert his rightness, an argument will ensue and the sale will be lost.

#2 (right way) Seller: "I see, well that is correct. When you first drive the car off the lot it does get the 38 highway, 34 city. Now as you drive it the gas mileage will go down and from what I have researched also you are correct. It also makes a difference how you drive the car and how well you keep up maintenance. If you keep the maintenance up regularly, drive it well, as in don't gun it, etc. you will get much better gas mileage."

This acknowledges the customer so they know they are understood, it doesn't compete with the customer but while making the seller right it also made the customer right. This will save the sale and shows that the salesperson understands the customer and respects him.

Try this sometime, talk to a friend about something you both know about but don't know "everything" about and try to accept everything they say even if you don't think it is correct. Watch how the conversation goes much smoother and you'll find you may learn something new.

Chapter Sixteen:

My finger slipped...

"Pull the trigger too soon and you can lose the sale."

You have probably heard this statement before. It is a widely used phrase in sales. However, how many people understand it? It simply means: if you try to close the sale before the customer is sold, you will lose the sale. Now this also works another way too. If you continue to try to sell the customer AFTER the point they are sold, you can also lose the sale.

When talking to a customer, if they are genuinely interested in the product, there will be a point in the sale that the customer is sold on the product and wants to buy it.

The customer may say something like, "I love it",

or "I'll take it." He might say something similar to this or he might not say anything at all but give a slight indication. This is up to you, as the seller, to catch that indication, even if only subtle, and close the sale. As your experience grows in this field you will become quicker and quicker at spotting that point. And at one point, it will become second nature.

You will be able to tell, just by looking at a customer whether they will buy the product or not. But, if you do not pay attention, you could lose many sales on this learning curve. So pay attention to your customers during the close and you'll have a much easier time.

Some examples of both:

"Pulling the trigger early"

Example:

> **Salesman:** *"So this car is a great car, gets good gas mileage and everyone seems to love it."*
>
> **Customer:** *"Well it's a nice car, I would like a little more information on it."*

> **Salesman:** *"Great! Let's go do the paperwork and you can drive it home today!"*

This customer likes the car, but is not ready to buy. The seller went right into the close assuming the customer was closed. This will not work. The customer would most likely get upset, or think the seller is incompetent. In this case, the seller could salvage the sale but would have to think on his feet.

> **Customer:** *"Uh, no I don't want to buy it right now. I just want more information."*
>
> **Salesman:** *"Oh, I am so sorry, I misunderstood. Let's go grab the spec sheets on the car and I can go over it with you and I can answer all your questions."*

The salesman has now taken responsibility for his mess up, handled the customer and has given the customer exactly what he wants. The salesman also remained in control by taking the customer to get the spec sheet.

These are examples of closing the sale before the customer is actually closed. This can be handled if done, but you have to have very good control and be very good at handling your customer.

Below is an example of the other side of this coin:

"Pulling the trigger too late!"

> **Customer:** *"Ok I'll take it."*
>
> **Salesman:** *"Great, now we do have this slightly larger package that I think you'll like. Here is what it is...(Shows bigger package)"*
>
> **Customer:** *"Oh that's nice too. You have given me something to think about."*

Customer walks away and you lost the sale. Very small chance the customer comes back.

Upselling is a good thing to do however it has to be done in the right way. We will go over that more later.

Here's a slightly different example but is all to common:

You are showing a pitch product, the customer, before you're done showing them the product asks for the price. Do you show them? Customers these days always want to know the price immediately. This has become automatic with most people, to immediately ask the price. The customer is not sold (exception to this is that they have bought the product before and are coming to buy more etc.). The handling for this is to get them back to the pitch, without showing them the price, but not ignore what they said:

> **Salesman:** *"So the product will help eliminate pest and ...."*
>
> (a lot of the times customers will interrupt you when they ask too)
>
> **Customer:** *"How much?"*
>
> **Salesman:** *"It's actually a very reasonable price, however let me show you one more thing that I think you'll really like."*

Salesman goes back into the pitch until he feels that the customer is closed. The customer is acknowledged and allows the seller to continue. Occasionally customers will ask again and again. If this occurs, handle the same way as above with different reasons.

If the customer continues to ask, show them the price, pause for a second to see if they respond or want to buy it, if not then continue the sale before they can leave or say no by getting them interested in the product again. (This will not usually occur, but as it does occasionally, this is how to handle it).

If you allow the customer to run the sale, you will likely lose the sale. In the example above, that is what the customer is trying to do by asking for the price before you are ready to give it to him.

The correct formula is, understand and return. Understand the objection or comment, and return to sales pitch.

Chapter Seventeen:

More or Less?

"Sell your customer what they want."

This one requires very little explanation, as it is self-explanatory. If you have a customer and they know what they want and are there to buy, sell them that.

Do not try and sell them too little or too much as you can lose the sale. Just sell them what they want. If it is a new customer and they are interested in buying something, sell them that or similar. As long as it's in the same range of what they want, it is ok.

Some sellers will try and sell a customer more or something the customer doesn't want. You will end up losing the sale and a customer.

If you have a customer who is ready to buy, sell them. They are ready to purchase. Close the sale! Do not continue because you can go past the point where the customer is sold.

Chapter Eighteen:

I swear..., True Story!

A little more on giving the customer stories. As we already went over this in chapter 14, Success Stories are a very good closing technique. After going through the entire sale and you're now at the point where the customer is deciding whether or not to buy it.

Sometimes they need a little more data. What data could you give them that you haven't already given them? Give them success stories. All companies should have a ton of success stories (if they're smart) that people have sent in raving about the product. Use them. If you know them by heart, tell the customer. Otherwise, have the customer read them.

The stories must be true and contain true data. Maintain your integrity. This will benefit you more in the long run. If you do not have any stories to tell, make sure that before you get a customer, to find some. Stories are one of the best closing tools. Most of the time they work the best after the customer has heard the pricing.

Chapter Nineteen:

"I'll think about it!"

Yep, that's the phrase that every sales person has heard more than enough times to last their lifetime, and then some. This phrase has become the nice way of saying "no" these days. If you're in sales, you probably hate this phrase. I have found that even people who do not speak English fully, know this phrase perfectly.

Now there are many versions of this phrase, but they all mean the same thing:

- "I'll think about it."
- "I'll be back."
- "I just got here."
- "I'm going to walk around and see what else I buy."

You get the idea.

However, these are just another way of saying, "no." Once you learn this you will be able to handle it much better. If a customer always told you exactly what was on their mind, sales would be a piece of cake. It would be the easiest profession to be in.

You would never waste your time on someone who was never going to close in the first place. You would probably close 95% of the people you talk to, not to mention, every single person in the world would be in sales.

This is not the case though. As a sales person you have to be able to understand what customers mean even when they do not say it exactly. Most of the time it is easier than it sounds but the above are the wide, well known phrases, which everyone hears. The way to handle it though, is extremely simple.

You simply: *Acknowledge the customer, and re-interest them in the product.*

When you master this, your sales will increase rapidly. The key though is to actually listen to the customer and handle them correctly.

Customer: *"Sounds good to me, I will think about it and come back."*

Sales Person: *"That's totally fine, what did you like about the product?"*

Customer said the all too familiar line. The sales person acknowledged the customer appropriately, and simply redirected the customer back into the conversation. Suddenly the customer is thinking about the product again and you're back on track.

Just remember, when a customer is trying to leave, or attempting to get off track, do not interrupt them if they're talking, but acknowledge them properly and redirect the conversation back to the correct route.

If they do end up leaving, make sure that they will remember you in a good way. Do not get mad at the customer, or "make yourself right." On the off chance that the customer does decide to come back, you want to make sure that he or she comes back to you! If you end the sale with the customer not buying, make sure they remember you in the best way, in case they do come back!

Chapter Twenty:

'Tag' me in.

"Tagging" is a term used in sales. It's a very valuable technique to use when a salesperson is working with a customer, and finds he needs to get some help closing the customer. The sales person excuses himself for a second to get another salesperson, or just calls another salesperson over, who is "fresh" or has information, which is important to this particular customer.

The new salesperson then helps the original salesperson close the sale. The reason this works so well is because the new salesperson comes in to the sale with a whole new energy and excitement.

Sometimes, if a salesperson is working with the same customer too long they can get "beat up." Bringing in a new salesperson helps jazz up the sales cycle and gets the customer excited again. The new salesperson also may have additional data, or stories that apply directly to this customer. Or they're simply a better "closer" than the original salesperson. Whatever it is, it works and is extremely valuable.

The thing about tagging that can actually mess up a sale is if the control is lost. If a salesperson attempts to tag with someone who didn't ask for it or expect it, it can throw off the entire sale. Whenever you're tagging, always let the original salesperson originate it, unless there is already a system worked out that will not ruin the sale.

As I said above, tagging is a great way to close sales, and if you get good at it, your sales will flourish!

Chapter Twenty-One:

Cash or Credit?

Closing is one of the, if not the biggest part in sales. The close is the point you feel the customer is sold. Where you stop and let the customer say they want to buy it.

Now closing can be messed up in many ways. A seller can talk too much and never fully "close", they could try and force the close, etc.

If you get to a close and the customer is not ready to buy it, a few things you can do are:

- Ask for the Sale.
- Give Success Stories
- Get them feeling the product if it is a tangible product and how they like it
- Ask them what they would use the product for or how it would benefit them.

"Asking for the sale"

This technique is so simple but it works 80% of the time and you would be surprised how many people do not do this. If a customer is closed but is not saying, "Yes I'll take it," or something of the sort, asking for the sale will close it.

> **Customer:** *"I like the product."*
>
> **Salesman:** *"Ok! Let's do it then!"*
>
> **Customer:** *"Ok!"*

Asking for the sale must be done at the close, it doesn't work any other time. Sometimes it is the close. It can also get the customer closed if they're on the fence. A lot of the time, people are afraid to make a decision. Help them make it by asking them to buy the product.

Other ways to ask: *"Want to go ahead with that?"* (Is a question but leads to a yes most of the time, or allows you to find out more data to sell them the product they need)

"So go ahead and get it so you can make sure to start using it immediately! You're going to love it!"

Anything similar to the above works. Pay attention to your questions at all times during sales. They should always lead to an agreement with you. Never ask a question that would get a negative response towards you or your product. You are always looking for agreement.

"Feeling the Tangible Product"

This may seem odd but it gets the customer liking the product. And creates more agreement with the product. Get them interacting with the product. In the sense of a cream or skin product, get them constantly feeling the place they put it on. If it's a hair product have them feel that.

If it's a car, have them play with the buttons, touch the outside, turn the wheel, test-drive the car, etc. As small as this seems, it is extremely valuable. It makes the customer "comfortable" with the product rather than making them feel like they are in completely new territory. It also gives them more control, personally, in this new environment.

"Ask them what they would use the product for or how it would benefit them."

If it is a product they would use, ask them how they would use it. How would it benefit them or make their life easier, etc. This puts the product in their mind and creates agreement with it. This will also get them thinking about how the product is valuable to them and that they would actually use it. As mentioned before, people who do not have a value created on a product will not buy it.

People are smart, they are not going to waste their money on something they don't want or do not see immediate value in. This is not saying that they will actually use it, but they will not buy it if they do not feel like they will use it. They need a reason why they should buy the product. It is your job to pull that reason out of them with your questions. And that's where the value comes into play.

Chapter Twenty-Two:

For just $40 more...!

Sales people are successful because they sell. Now everyone, as you have learned at this point can sell. They just need to be taught. So what makes the difference between an average seller and the above average seller? The upsell.

When a customer is closed, and they are buying the product, this is the only time to try and upsell. Here is the key; the customer must be in the process of buying the product. You have their credit card, or their paperwork etc. At this point, if you feel comfortable that you could possibly upsell them, try.

Remember, their paperwork is done, or you have their credit card, or whatever your specific closing point is. If the customer likes the product, and you feel like they would buy more, try to upsell them. The worse that happens is they say "no" and you finish the original sale. But a lot of times you can talk them into a slightly larger sale, especially if they really like the product and if they originally closed easily.

Just make sure you have their form of payment for the original sale first. If you allow them to think too much about the upsell, you could lose the original sale, because remember, if you "oversell" the customer you can lose the sale. Don't get me wrong. This has happened to me before, but 99 times out of 100, the upsell worked, or they bought the original sale.

If you want to be the best sales person you can be, never forget the upsell!

Chapter Twenty-Three:
"My dad's better than your dad!"

Another key thing in sales is the way you present yourself to customers. Being the best doesn't mean going around and telling people you are the best. You can tell people anything, doesn't mean they will believe you. You have to prove yourself time and time again, especially these days.

Ways to discredit yourself immediately are:

- *Dressing down and not looking professional.*
- *Talking bad about other companies, whether competing or not.*
- *Talking bad about customers at any point in time.*

- *In pitch products, having a bad demonstration or an unorganized demonstration location, etc.*

These are just a few examples of how you can discredit yourself, and your product/company quickly.

If you are selling a product which you believe in and like selling, you do not have to do anything but interest the customer in the product and you will sell. Look professional, have an organized area for demonstration or customer relations. Keep your product clean and presentable. These are things that are so simple but will benefit you so much.

A lot of people believe that talking bad about competitors will work in their favor. The funny thing is, it is the complete opposite. Here's what happens, the customer goes to the competitors to check it out for themselves.

You have officially interested the customer in the other product rather than just selling yours. Big no-no. Now, not only have you lost a customer, but also, they probably bought your competitors product.

If a customer asks you: "What's the difference between your product and theirs?" The worst thing to do is say, "Oh, well theirs is this, that and the other thing, and ours is better because of this, that and the other thing."

The customer will now go look at the other product. If you said one thing that wasn't true, you lost the sale and your credibility. It's sort of a double-edged sword when it comes to this. If a customer asks you what the difference is between your product and your competition, and you tell them how bad the competitors is, often, they won't trust you again.

You talked bad about another product, and people don't like to buy from a guy who puts someone else down. It's a very interesting phenomena but I see it every day. (Personally, I have found that the only type of people bad mouthing works on is the types who complain about others also. And guess what, they will also complain about you after they leave, whether you make the sale or not.)

The correct handling when a customer asks you the difference is to say, "You know, I am not 100% sure. However, ours does this, that and the other thing (bringing their attention back to your product). From what you have told me, you like these features. Ours has all of them and I can even add this one for free!" A statement like this or similar (depending on your product) will work great!

It keeps their attention on your product and does not allow for any other thoughts. It is the best way to handle this situation. The moral of the story is to stick to your own product. Do not worry about competitors. If you're product is good, you will sell it. No need to complicate things.

Another big point in sales is to dress appropriately. If you are selling a good product and want to look the part, you have to dress the part. People respect a man or woman who looks professional. If you are selling a product but you're wearing ripped jeans and a t-shirt, you probably won't get much respect. Remember, you are representing your product. Don't you want it to be represented well?

This does have another side. Yes, you want to dress professionally, but you also want to dress to your public. If you are selling high-end software to business owners, you do not want to look trashy, you want to look professional. However, what if your public is skateboarders. Would you dress in slacks and a button up?

Probably not. It wouldn't be appropriate. You would want to wear nice jeans and a T-Shirt, or a button up. You need to dress to relate with your customers.

In conclusion, dress the part, represent your product, keep the focus and watch your sales soar!

Chapter Twenty-Four:

Homework!

A lot of people in sales are good at sales because they are good at talking to people; they aren't shy on approaching people and they can handle conflict. However, there is one important thing that is constantly over looked: Knowing what you are selling!!!

When you first start selling something, you will not know everything. You will learn what you are taught in training but all companies want to get you selling immediately and will mostly teach you the basics. This leaves it up to you to continue learning. Do research, define words you don't understand relating to the product or similar products, learn about competing products, the differences, similarities, get current customer successes, what they liked about the product, what they didn't like about it and why, etc.

The reason to learn about the product is simple but rarely applied. If you are talking to a customer and they ask you a question, you should know the answer, you're selling the product. If you can't answer it, you look silly. Or worse, you try and bullshit the answer, and if the customer knows anything, you make yourself look stupid along with the company.

Learn, study, and research. Do these things when selling a product and your sales will increase dramatically. Most companies have lots of information on their product and will be happy to help you learn more.

One of the biggest mistakes to make in sales is to give a fake or uncertain answer. If a customer asks, "How does this do …." and you give them a fake or bullshit answer, a couple things can happen. If the customer knows anything about the product or situation they're asking about, you would instantly be called out and probably lose the sale, making you look stupid as well as the company.

The best handling when a customer asks you a question you do not know the answer to is so simple. Just be honest. A customer responds so well to honesty. If you are honest with a customer over something you don't know they will trust you more in the long run. This is because these days, customers are so skeptical because of all the fake advertisement, manipulated phrases etc.

A simple example of this is car commercials. In the commercial you see the really hot model, with all the features, upgrades and extras. Then at the end it says, "starting at $$$$." So they show you the highest model but show you the lowest price, the "starting Price." This is a mild example but you'll start to notice things like that if you start paying attention.

Example (you are selling T.V.s):

WRONG WAY FIRST

Customer: *"What is the difference between Brand X and Brand B?"*

Seller: (who has just started and hasn't had much training) *"Well Brand X has a high capacity output and more pixels. It also has more connections so you can connect all of your game systems, sound systems etc. Brand B is not as fast but has more color output."*

Now what the seller said sounds good to anyone who really doesn't know much about TVs, and could potentially sound correct. However it doesn't give exact data and let's say the customer knows something about TVs. The seller now looks silly, not to mention the data is incorrect.

The correct way to handle this is to:

> **Seller:** *"Honestly I just started and I am not 100% sure about the differences. However let me go get someone to help with that question (or they could just go find out). While I find out please look at the visual difference. I really think Brand X has a much nicer picture than Brand B though."*

This shows the seller has integrity and shows the customer that the seller cares enough about the customer to get the correct answer and make sure their needs are taken care of. This is a very important point in sales. Be Honest!

Make sure to always keep learning about the product you are selling. You can never have too much knowledge about your product. You can always learn. The more you know, the more you will sell!

Chapter Twenty-Five:

Who are you?

A lot of people think that if they emulate successful sales people they themselves will be successful and this is true to some degree. However, each person is different from the next and some things that one person does, that would be successful for them, may not be successful for another person. The important thing is to find the basic technique that they are applying and adapt it to you.

You can apply all the data above and still not sell. You could talk to a customer who has walked in to buy, with their credit card in hand ready to buy and actually turn that person around. How? By being or emulating someone else.

This will be harder for some people to grasp as some people do this automatically and don't even notice that they are trying to act like someone else, or do something that someone else is doing.

Everyone is different to some degree; the key is using your unique-ness to your advantage. By being yourself, and applying the data above in your own way you will find that you will sell much better than trying to be "Joe Shmo, who is the best seller around."

I have been in sales for a long time, and a lot of people say, "I want to be as good as you." My response is, "You will never be me, you can be better than me!" And that is the truth. Everyone has the potential to be a phenomenal seller. They just have to find what works for them.

In sales, if you are yourself, have fun and apply the above data, you will find you do better overall, in life and professionally.

Chapter Twenty-Six:

Additional Data

Remember, sales are not hard. I have seen, and trained practically every type of person you can imagine to sell well. The points in this book are basic, but if applied will help you become a great salesperson. I do hope it helps you.

Just remember sales are basic.

- *Receive Customer*
- *Enlighten the customer on your product*
- *Close the customer.*

Of course, inside all of that is more involved, however that's how basic sales are. Below is a list to help you remember the chapters in this book.

One of my favorite things to tell people is:

"I'm not a salesman, I just enlighten you, and you make the decision to buy it!"

I do hope this helps you become the best salesperson you can be! Remember, as a salesperson, you always have new stuff to learn, so keep learning!

Here's to a lot of sales and a never-ending supply of customers!

Chapter Twenty-Seven:

Cheat Sheet

Set high targets every day and week and actually shoot for them. Do not shoot for a bare minimum. If you beat your targets don't stop! Keep Selling! (Chapter 1)

Keep your attention on the customers. (Chapter 2)

The more customers you talk to, the more success you'll have. (Chapter 3)

Be Energetic and happy. Smile! (Chapter 4)

Frustration will be the end of you. (Chapter5)

Be positive, and have good body language. (Chapter 6)

Demonstrate your product. Customers like to see. (Chapter 7)

Be interested in them, not interesting to them. (Chapter 8)

Create interest and value with the customer. (Chapter 9)

Find the key reason and the rest will fall into place (Chapter 10)

Control the sale and conversation. (Chapter 11)

Keep the conversation on the product. Do not go on tangents. (Chapter 12)

Giving compliments is a very valuable tool. (Chapter 13)

Give true data, not made up opinions. (Chapter 14)

"Being right" will lose sales. (Chapter 15)

Pull the trigger too soon, and lose the sale. (Chapter 16)

Sell customers what they want, not more or less. (Chapter 17)

Stories, not lies, are extremely beneficial in closing. (Chapter 18)

Consider any customer who "is going to come back" or "will think about it" will not be a sale. Close now! (Chapter 19)

Tagging is a great way to help get closes. (Chapter 20)

Don't be afraid to ask for the sale! (Chapter 21)

When closed, don't be afraid to upsell! (Chapter 22)

Dress the part, and keep the focus. No bad-talking competitors. (Chapter 23)

Continue to learn your product and you will continue to sell better and better. (Chapter 24)

Be yourself and have fun! (Chapter 25)

About the Author

William J. Simpson IV has been both a salesman and a sales trainer since the early 2000's and draws his techniques from a cross section of various industries. He prides himself on endeavoring to be the best at his profession and through his instruction of others seeks to impart those same ideals. His success comes from breaking down the sales experience, imparting his simplified approach and sharing battle tested techniques he has learned over a decade. He currently travels the country instructing, speaking and training others on his methods. He lives in Clearwater, Florida.

www.IfAndorButPublishing.com

www.ingramcontent.com/pod-product-compliance
Lightning Source LLC
Chambersburg PA
CBHW020925180526
45163CB00007B/2884